In Search of Warm Breathing Things

poems by
Katherine Gekker

Glass Lyre Press

Copyright © 2019 Katherine Gekker
Paperback ISBN: 978-1-941783-61-0

All rights reserved: except for the purpose of quoting brief passages for review, no part of this book may be reproduced or transmitted in any form or by any means, electronic or mechanical, including photocopying, recording, or by any information storage and retrieval system, without permission in writing from the publisher.

Author Photo: Lianna Gekker
Design & Layout: Steven Asmussen
Cover Art: Katherine J. Williams
Copyediting: Linda E. Kim

Glass Lyre Press, LLC
P.O. Box 2693
Glenview, IL 60025
www.GlassLyrePress.com

In Search of Warm Breathing Things

for Mariah

Contents

One

Past Tense	1
Time Will Tell	2
Sweet Chocolate	3
We Do Not Know the Words	4
Beluga Pangaea	6
Day of Beauty: Facial	8

Two

The World Trembles, The World Masquerades	11
Ice Waterfall	12
To Cast a Shadow Again	13
Now, Four Blizzards	17
Labyrinth	19
Rutting Fall	21
Grammar's Emotional Rules	23
Alcohol Beckons Constantly, Derails	25
Trauma, Printing Company	26
Inside a Coffee Shop	27
Ocean Dawn	28
Refracted Light	29
Smoke	30

Three

Solving for the Unknown	33
Number(s) Theory	34
What the Brochure Promises	36
Near Meander River, Near Miletus	38
A Grackle Writes a Poem	39
Coco Eats Breakfast	40
Midnight Garden Walk, Key West	41
Nature's Cadenza	42
In Search of Warm Breathing Things	44

Four

Butterfly Poster, Printing Company	47
Morning Shift, Printing Company	48
1968, Memorial Chapel, Ohio	49
Vietnam Summer Friends, 1969	50
Cherry Tree Kabuki	52
Our Frozen Forest Walk	53
Scar in the Moon	54
The Dog Hates Storms	55
Overnight Maples Turn into Pumpkins	56
Last Walk	57
September – Arlington, Virginia	58

Acknowledgments	61
About the Author	63

One

Past Tense

1.

You begin to speak of me
in the past tense –

>   *Who were you?*
>   *I don't know what you believed.*

As if to know and to let go
are simultaneous events.

As if I am the one leaving.

2.

On your first day of school it rained.
Someone took a picture of you
thin beneath your leather satchel, your beret.
The black and white photo
makes you look forever
gray with anticipation.

3.

Beneath cryptomeria, a lone cypress,
we sow your ashes.
Kneeling, we fold them
into the soil.
They gleam against dark earth.

Our eyelashes glow silver
in the night's mist.

This is who I was –
          a girl in the rain at night.

Time Will Tell

Time will tell this is the last
        hurricane. Willows swoop, bow

down, branches brush earth, elongated
        leaves prostrate till trunks jerk

upright and boughs snap like flags, then
        bend low again, acts of devotion, obedient

to the wind. From behind tall windows,
        we are like tourists watching

pilgrims circle Potala Palace. They
        kneel, extend clappers, spread limbs

until completely prone, rise again to inch forward.

We cannot see the wind. We only see what
        the wind does. We say, look at that wind.

I eat my lunch, you sip the one spoonful
        of broth you can manage today, you

shift in your seat, wicker creaks, I ask *are you*
        in pain? You ask *why do you keep looking at me?*

I look out at the wind. I can see
        the wind, and what time will tell.

Sweet Chocolate

*They said there'd be
chocolate*, you tell me
on the last day
you are able to speak.

Your eyes widen, look
deliberately at the table
where they leave your meals.

You are too weak
to move your head,
stopped chewing weeks ago,
no longer swallow.
Nurses swab morphine
inside your mouth.

I no longer eat either.
But before leaving home
this morning, I put
five Hershey's Kisses
in my purse. So I say
They are right.
There is chocolate.

I place one morsel in your
mouth. After a long
time your thin neck
swallows. Your last meal.

Your eyelids close
slowly, carefully.
That is how you thank me.

After a while, you say,
If I'm smiling the next
time you see me, you'll
know what has happened.

We Do Not Know the Words

We watch our mother's every breath.
Her gaze is fixed, but not on us.

We do not know the words
for where we are about to go.

> Jibs furl, jibs
> unfurl. We sail in
> shallows, escape
> shoals. Tentacles
> beckon us to
> dive, sound our
> depths. The octopus
> seeks whatever we
> are seeking.

We can only say the words we can say.
We only have the language we already have.

> We reckon our position
> each noon. Astrolabes,
> sextants tell us
> nothing we want
> to know except
> where we are at
> noon. Fathoms
> below, light
> curves a new
> geometry, fluid
> shifts on the
> depths we sound.

We know she breathes by the rising of her chest.
Her gaze is fixed, but not on us.

We can only say the words we can say.
We only have language for what we know.

We will learn the words
for where we all eventually go.

Beluga Pangaea

1.

Our guide sounds the gathering note.
    The boat leans as we all rush to see.

Outside, colors chatter, confuse
    in gray water, gray light. Are those
        whitecaps or belugas? Mothers or
            their gray blue calves?

Wind hisses across the foam –
    a duet with sea canaries'
        coloratura whistles, clicks
            rising to the descant.

Whales slip around, over, under each
    other. Mothers' hydrocephalic heads crest
        while their small shadows curve,
            weave, unwilling to separate.

2.

Each year belugas migrate thousands
    of miles south. Each year they return to
        this estuary where marine and riverine waters
            mix. Grown calves swim again with their mothers

until the old whales slip
    away as the old do,
        sinking quietly past the krill.

3.

I dreamed this dream when
    my mother was still living:

She is driving away from me, slowly.
She signals to me through the window,
a private, loving gesture known only to us.

Day of Beauty: Facial

The attendant knots a towel
around my face to hold my
chin and hair in place –

>	like the towel the nurses
>	wrapped around my mother's
>	face to keep her jaw from
>	dropping, as if we cared about that –

crosses my hands on my chest,
wraps a blanket around me –

>	like the sheet the nurses
>	wrapped around my mother
>	after they crossed her hands on her chest,
>	so she looked like she was praying,
>	as if they needed to make her
>	presentable, as if she weren't already
>	beautiful, her face
>	thin like a girl's.

When they brought the gurney
to take my mother away, we all helped
wind her into that sheet, and finally
covered her face, so we never saw her again,
so that the last touches she had
were from those she loved.

Today the attendant wraps
me and turns me and
touches me. Tells me –
This is a day of beauty.

Two

The World Trembles, The World Masquerades

        May, acid green like a new
    snake, past scorched August
           into September bursting orange,
I played around, strayed from you, belovéd.
      A new love put a spell on me, promised
         – oh, the promises – if only I would
    leave you behind –

                would you even know or care?
      Then October's early morning light
    slanted, frost gleaming on crisped
grass. Fog smoked, dallied over a pond,
      dread winter hovered. I shivered, a hand
        lingered on my shoulder, a touch so light
    it didn't warm me.

              Something – an airborne
      jellyfish? transparent skate? – shimmered,
    skimmed invisible waves, flew at me, I
couldn't take my eyes off it – it
      dazzled, glittered, I stepped aside to avoid –
        a spider's web – threads glinting,
    gliding from their anchor into this net

      of the wind's choosing. I turned, watched
the filament float by, disappear. No one else
    noticed anything – I wondered why –

      Then I remembered who I am and
    then I remembered who
can I tell this to but you?

Ice Waterfall

The dog's been underfoot all day,
you say.
You two need a walk.

Banished, the dog and I
hike toward the river
away from the wind
away from that chilling phone call.
No one else is out.

Above us, waterfalls are ice –
one wave frozen in its tumble
over the edge.
Patiently it waits for a gentler season
unlike my friend who
slipped a rope over
her head and stepped
off a stool.

The sun sets with winter abruptness.
We turn toward home.
A flock of black birds
with much ado and chatter
settles in for the night.
The dog hurries, eager
to be underfoot again.

Tears sting my eyes.
Is it the sharp wind,
or the glimpse of you
in the kitchen?
Across the frozen field between us
yellow light spills
like buttercups.

To Cast a Shadow Again

1.

Stopped by the stream
we steam like two workhorses.

The moisture lies white
on the field
and your shoulders.

Our own fog melts
thin shingles of ice water.

I lean over to kiss
your halo of moisture.

My face comes away wet.

2.

Luminescent moonlight startles me –
I'm wildly awake in the wrong season.

Your foot hangs out of the covers
and like a lighthouse for the moon
directs its rays to a safe landing.
There's a pulse on your instep.

Everything else is night
but your foot, the moon, my eyes.

What woke me –
the whiteness of your skin.

3.

Two bees are fighting or courting –
I can't tell which.

The ground's covered with flowers
smooth as kid leather bats' wings.

We sit surrounded, our backs hard
against the tulip magnolia.

Your words drift down
like blossoms around my ears.

4.

That didn't take too long –
I thought I was asleep. But
your hand –
currents over my hip.

Five seconds
changed the color of leaves
the smell of earth
the shapes of stars.

I'm awake now, always.
The moon is company. Its only comfort –
a blue whiteness on my body
where I long for your hand to cast a shadow again.

5.

Everyone says it snowed last night
but I know it's the whitening of your love
blowing across my eyelids
where your lips used to rest.

A confused tree sends out one green branch,
covets its few withered leaves and won't release them to the snow.
Not evergreen, but half green –
like us.
Our feet kick up white storms.
Wet ankles skim over the trails.

This is what I want to hold –
one green branch on a hibernating tree.
It bent softly when I brushed against it.

6.

Hands underwater on my body –
gentle fingers flutter
frictionless, like fish
brush against me
and quick swim away.
Waves chop.

Your hands can't rest, they find no purchase.
I'm about to go under.

You only touched me once under water
but this is how I remember it always –
your hands slide away.

7.

Cordite surrounded you.
Caps popped in my heart
that day we held fireballs in our mouths –
red tongues   dangerous drums –

Our small battles squealed Roman candles.

Now you march
across the street to me
through a haze of gunpowder –
Battalion guarding my heart fortress.

8.

Lie down and cry
and tears will roll into your ears.

Your words, my words, blank ceiling,
and my ears are wet, cold.
Your words did that to me.

Now, Four Blizzards

1.

The radio interrupts old songs, warns –
>   *Severe winter storm!*
>   *Extremely hazardous conditions* –
but you drive fast
into onslaughting snow.

Flakes like flashing stars
aim for my eyes,
divide at the windshield at the last moment.

The blizzard bends around us
like time through space.

2.

You drive at the speed of light
into dark, our convertible
hurtles away from the sun
in a blizzard of neutrinos.

When you turn on the headlamps,
their beams fade into night.
We're a star shimmering in the past,
listening to songs we cannot remember –

3.

Except this: a blizzard disappeared
into the ocean, rimed the ship's edges
white with ringing, stopped all thought
where metal ends.

The ship groaned, then dipped
so we saw only water,
a dark wall above us, dark
except for reflected white and red beams,
reflections of the ship's running lights.

This light vanished long ago.

4.

Everything quickens around you –
surf rushes our feet.
Ice, sand, feldspar sting our skin.

Snow melts in the ocean,
stirs sand with hoary frost
until waves drown the whiteness.

The blizzard salts your
shoulders, your eyelashes.
I can't catch my breath.

The world bends toward us,
the world bends away.

Everywhere I look is dark.

A wild song vibrates through dunes,
disappears in hissing foam.

Labyrinth

Island ferry – giddy day-trippers,
      high spirits – almost like our
honeymoon. We giggle, hold hands,
      reminisce. You pack our mopeds –
sandwiches, your beer, my soda.

We weave across roads, lean low
      over handlebars, pretend we're
motorcycle racers. At the narrow
      shoal, we ditch mopeds,
chase each other over Great Dune

to the sound where dolphins glide
      like mercury. You call to me,
open your arms wide. Your
      collarbones shimmer like wings,
gleam in the sun's light. Your face

is shadowed, dark. You fret –
      *There won't be time to buy
more beer before the last ferry.*
      I want to walk the labyrinth
cut in the meadow between sound

and ocean. *It'll take just a minute,*
      I say. My hurried steps startle
burying beetles, muslin moths.
      Porcupine grasses scratch my legs.
I worry about poison ivy, snakes.

A sign says *Discard anything
      you want to let go of
at the labyrinth's center.* I see
      crumpled cigarette packs,
a photo, folded slips of paper.

I leave nothing behind, but I
        walk the labyrinth over and over.
You march toward me, kick
        at brambles, furious. Tiny
insects flutter, dizzy in your wake.

Let's GO, you snarl.
                      You're drunk,
    I say, something I have never said
to you. Then you call me that word.

Rutting Fall

1.

A deer clatters onto the macadam,
        catapults against a car, booms
    like a blown transformer, ricochets
white-tail over antlers into a guardrail,
        then stops moving.

Beside Clifton Forge, Divided
        Fork, Rocky Branch, beneath
    pewter skies, trees colored
copper, bronze, brass,
        deer keep breaking their bodies
in a headlong race toward
        passion, a rutting need to run.

2.

I taste metal as if chewing a fender
        whenever I remember how I stepped
    away from you last summer, off a curb
and into traffic, yanked back by a stranger
    who saw the truck before I did. The truck
sped by me so close my clothes flapped
        in its wind stream.
                      I was grateful
for that breeze on my burning skin. Later
        you told me I looked like a scarecrow,
    tottering between street
and safety, one arm held by a stranger,
    one leg in the air, and you said
I looked through you as if nothing
        had happened.

3.

Every fall, our dog chased deer, ran
        till we could no longer see or hear him.
    Just when we began to worry
that he had run onto a highway,
    he'd prance toward us,
his coat the same color as fallen
        leaves, leaves so dry they rattled
as we kicked through them,
    rattled as if they were bones.

He died on a metal table, his eyes
        watching us till the end, his legs
    thin as a deer's, his white feathers still
gleaming against his golden coat.

I tell you – *Now that the dog is gone,*
there's no reason to come home.

Grammar's Emotional Rules

1. Progressive Forms (Adjectives and Adverbs)

Angry, angrier, angriest:
    positive, comparative, superlative forms.

    Ex. I'm positively angry that you don't pay attention to me.

Always use comparatives and superlatives with care.

    Ex. I'm comparatively angrier day by day
        because you go out drinking.

    Ex. I'm superlatively the angriest I've ever been
        because you just called me that awful word
        because I just called you a drunk.

2. Misplaced Limiting Modifiers

Just is a limiting modifier.
Anger can be just –

    Ex. Just anger, as in simple anger,
        as in I'm just angry that you drink every night.

        or

    Just anger, as in righteous anger,
    as in I'm joining the Women's Temperance Society
    because people like you are ruining my life and the lives
        of others.

Misplaced anger is never a misplaced modifier.
Anger is difficult to modify.

Anger can be limiting
but do not limit your anger.

You should limit your drinking,
but I'm allowed to be as angry as I want.

3. Count and Noncount Nouns, Both Proper and Common

Anger counts, always.
Anger can be proper
if you don't become a harridan.
If you become a harridan,
anger is common.

Anger always arrives in degrees,
but anger is not always positive.
I exceed all others in anger.
I am positive about that.

Alcohol Beckons Constantly, Derails

each and every day earlier and earlier. Your breakfast juice –
firewater, which means forlorn me, followed by medicinal
gimlet. You're ginned up long before cocktail
hour, hosed by metallic vodka,
ice cubes clinking against cut crystal, those
jazz jezebels jockey with your reason. Your mind, the whole
kit and caboodle, goes kablooey. You say,
let the drinking begin. I say, *you lush, it never stops, look in the
mirror – that's you smashed by margaritas.*
Not that you drink indiscriminately. No, you nurse
only one rule – keep drinking. You
pour another, pursue your pickled
quest, a quagmire of doctored quinine.
Righteous, rigid, ruined in rum, you're
sloshed, snookered by Scotch,
trashed, tumbled under the table,
useless. You're
vacant, veer away from me, seek vermouth –
weeping, whiskey-wasted, wankered. I long to be an
ex,
yearn to unyoke from you, you
zonked zombie. Soon, I will swing from
                               a crystal
                        chandelier,
                catapult
              through the
      open
window and disappear into the night: Zorro –
    No.

                    Zorra!

Trauma, Printing Company

Suddenly a gear grabs
        my wedding ring, reels
my hand into the press.

At the hospital they tell me
        Your nerves have been damaged.
Three doctors struggle
        to remove the ring.
Just cut it off I scream.
        They promise *We can save it.*

When the anesthesia wears off,
        I come to alone. Later
they slip the band onto my
        right finger with a tenderness
I barely recognize.

Inside a Coffee Shop

I see your face reflect away from
     mine in the window. At last night's
dinner, you never once

     looked at me. Finished, you folded
your napkin exactly at its
     creases, shrugged, said *Well*.

My knee jiggles under the table.
     I am almost as angry
as that man whose book I just read.

     "Stairway to Heaven" repeats
a third time. How do we keep
     arriving at this same place?

Outside, light shifts, blazes.
     Seven steel stabiles rise, fall
yet remain on the same plane.

     Infinite loops rotate. Shapes like
open palms say hello,
     goodbye, sit down, be quiet.

Ocean Dawn

Surf thunders in time
with your breath, your pulse,
then disappears in whispering foam.

Feathered white moths
beat a tattoo
against streetlamps.

We've made it through
our last night.
We won't rise together again.

At dawn, moths disappear upward
toward more compelling light.

Gray and pink skies streak the ocean
platinum, gold, rose.
Outer light is not insight; it is illusion.

Once you told me –
> *Don't complicate things.*
> *It's not so hard to separate.*

Refracted Light

1. Coda

That light loops endlessly.
Older than sound
it happens long ago.
It doesn't affect anyone now.

2. Kitchen, 2 a.m.

The bottle sounds like a bell
    when it bumps against the tumbler.
You say it's water,
    I say it's gin, its platinum
ice cubes refract light
    into spider webs of rainbows.
        You spit out some words.

3. Pool, 8 a.m.

Light slips like minnows through water,
    dissolves in ripples at the pool's bottom.
My strokes crack the surface's membrane.
    Their ostinato creates waves
that boomerang against the edge
    bounce back at me, bobbing
        like a bottle in the middle of the ocean.

4. Coda

That light loops endlessly.
Older than sound
it happens long ago.
It doesn't affect anyone now.

Smoke

We move like ghosts through the trees
this gray spring morning,
my coat as wet as the dog's.
A bright goldfinch flies across our path,
startles us –

like your name in this morning's newspaper
after all these years
startles me.
They mention our failed marriage.
Misspell my name.

The dog and I climb the hill home.
Suddenly the wind blows.
I smell cigarette smoke.
The dog growls, ears up.
I look around –
only shadows in the woods.

I remember you crossed the street
in front of my car
one summer day so bright
I almost couldn't see you,
so hot you shimmered
like the smoke from your cigarette.
I caught my hand mid-gesture
waving to you.
You walked over,
appeared more solid as you got closer.
How could I know then
I would never see you again?

Three

Solving for the Unknown

Poetry class starts at 7:30. I arrive at 7:15.
    Parking costs 25 cents for 30 minutes.
        Meters are enforced till 10. Class ends
    at 9:45. When I spot classmates, I casually
disclose, *I left my watch at home. I've put 27*

quarters in the meter — is that enough? Each
    week I find a different person to ask. I buy
        rolls of quarters at the bank. The teller
    can't tell me how many quarters I need.
She says she doesn't understand poetry. Meter

maids patrol the lot, ticket the scofflaws, extract
    clattering coins from machines. I insert 5
        quarters into my parking meter, their
    drop systolic rhythm, their sequence iambic
pentameter. They race through dark pipes like

cells raced through my mother's glands. When
    our father died, my brother and I lost one
        quarter of our family. When our mother
    died, one third of our family was gone. Now
here I am stuffing quarters into a slot, calculating.

Number(s) Theory

1. Odd / Even

>1 is odd.
>13 is odd.
>137 is odd.
>1370 is even.
>
>Zero = nothing.
>Nothing is even.
>What is even stays even.
>What is odd stays odd
>
>except when zeroed.
>Zero makes everything even.

2. Addition / Subtraction

>Addition: numbers combine to increase value.
>Subtraction: numbers combine to lose value.
>Addition or subtraction = change, more or less.
>
>Except zero adds nothing
>and zero subtracts nothing.
>
>Nothing from nothing leaves nothing.

3. Numbers / People

>People can be even.
>For instance, you and I together are even.
>People can be odd.
>For instance, you and I and that other person = odd.
>
>People add themselves or
>take themselves away.

People cannot be zero
except when someone becomes zero.

That always follows subtraction.

4. Numbers / Place

Our street number is 1370.
Is our house on the even or odd
side of the street?
(See 1. Odd / Even.)

5. Answers

We live on the even
side of the street

although, oddly, you
are no longer even there so
we are no longer even together.

Therefore, I am now
1, alone, and thus odd
in more ways than
numbers can count.

What the Brochure Promises

*Unlock the beauty hidden
in common rocks,*
the brochure promises.
*Anyone can operate
this inexpensive machine to
release minerals' healing powers.*

The basement rumbles,
squeaks. The dog suspects
mice, races downstairs, overturns
paint cans, jars of nails
in his frenzied hunt.
I assure him – *it's only
the rock tumbler.*

My chest vibrates,
sometimes my heart stutters.
I watch my pulse beat
in my blue wrists.

Does my left arm tingle, grow numb?
I'm always angry.

Yesterday, another test –
a cold steel wand
amplified watery
sounds, projected
a trembling fist
on a gray screen. Each
chamber pulsed like a blowfish.

My heart began to jump.
Three doctors gathered around the screen.
Already people talk about me
as if I am no longer here.

An almost full moon hangs
low in the sky, slightly out of
round.
           It's time –
open the rock tumbler, rinse
the stones, add fresh water,
the final polishing sand.

The brochure promises –
    In 72 hours, the stones
    will emerge smooth and finished –
        lustrous jewels.

Near Meander River, Near Miletus

A blue tiller's curved prongs
    rust toward red in some
        farmer's abandoned
field. One beetle crawls
    along a scarred furrow, a doughboy
in a trench, no way to turn around,
    no way to climb out,
        the only way – forward.

Each step limits the next
    step's choice
        or expands it, temple
or field, fallen columns
    and ruined gods –
these are and are not dialectics here
    in Meander's alluvium.

Ruins surround us,
    thin dogs prowl a barren
        tourist stop, its
oranges, warm coke, no
    temptation.

For the first time in my life
    I part my hair on the left,
        stumble past myself,
unrecognizable, in mirrors. No one here
    knows me, including me.
I need to lie in wait to see myself.

One coriander- and cumin-stained
    chickpea lies on the ancient
        soil. If I were hungrier
I would pick it up.

A Grackle Writes a Poem

My only rooftop companion –
one grackle, iridescent –
splashes through a puddle,
a puddle so shallow it cannot cover the bird's feet.

The grackle frolics while I sit.
Each hop breaks this surface.
I almost wrote hope, not hop.

I don't want to write certain words –
alone or lonely, for instance.

I don't want to write.
I don't want to call the puddle a tiny lake.
I don't want to describe the puddle's rainbow-oil surface.
I want to look at this puddle,
keep company with this lone grackle.

Perhaps my grackle can describe
how obsidian surfaces break, disturb
clouds reflected in shallow puddles.

Coco Eats Breakfast
– for Condavi

Coco the palm warbler wears
chartreuse against her
gray and brown body, her
eyebrow pencil a bright yellow.
Tiny, lithe, she is the avian
Audrey Hepburn of Key West.

Her breakfast, served on a white
plate on the picnic table
beneath orchid-filled palms –
Old Town Bakery's crusty
walnut bread; Fausto's hard goat
cheese, ecru with a thin brown vein
of truffle, smelling of earth, autumn;
and, most prized, one grub.

Before she dares peck at her food,
Coco's head darts side to side,
her glass black eyes like a frightened doll.
Sylvester the catbird, twice her size,
might swoop back any moment.

One clump of feathers, stained dark blood,
sticks out near Coco's liver.
She does not speak of what happened.

Midnight Garden Walk, Key West

One palm rat whispers along
     fence slats, slightly
          ahead of a patient rat snake.
I place my bare feet carefully.

Wind shuffles palm fronds –
     they swoop, stripe the path,
          they stripe the low sky.
This storm feels like the start
     of a hurricane, but it's only

simple wind, simple rain.
     My shift billows, diaphanous.
          I am dancing in Isadora Duncan's

scarves, Salomé's. I can
     seduce anyone tonight beneath
          fronds like slicing blades.

Nature's Cadenza
– inspired by John Cage's 4'33"

    1st movement

Eastern timber rattler's percussive clicks
    crescendo   decrescendo

Bird's song like a cell phone ring tone
like the sound of your cell phone
when I wasn't the one calling

Don't let your cageless ear
become your caged mind

    2nd movement

Listen:

: chlorophyll escapes,
turns poison ivy leaves crimson

: red-eyed green tree frogs dig deep
    into pond-damp mud

: they won't escape the silent cottonmouth's
    fanged white jaws

I was every subject but yours

    3rd movement

Nature's cadenza:

: the owl's wings beat a midnight ostinato

: the copperhead's thick body flattens turf,
    then grass blades spring up,
        freed in its vibrato wind stream

: the mouse cringes, its fur quivers –
    heart beat's frantic tremolo

Feel sound waves lift my wild hair,
    bypass my wild ears

        the silence; the sound

In Search of Warm Breathing Things

A snapping turtle breaststrokes forward.
    Nails clatter loud on macadam,
        his spiked tail whipsaws.

Behind his big biting head, dried
    mud cakes the turtle's checkerboard
        shell, its edges eaves of a pagoda.

He startles me – daydreaming on my walk –
    still half asleep after thrashing
        all night in a too-big bed,

my mind rehashing old arguments.
    When another creature bellows
        from a nearby pond – deep,

echoing – my turtle turns his head,
    plops off the path.
        Feet sawmill through air –

he slides down a bank, sinks
    into mud next to a mate.
        Side by side, snouts in the air,

two scaly necks vibrate, two
    rough voices sing in unison.
        Later tonight it might be too quiet to

sleep, the bed again too empty.
    Or perhaps I will not be able to sleep
        for the sound of singing.

Four

Butterfly Poster, Printing Company

Make them look alive,
says the customer.

All day long the cylinders roll –
sheets of butterflies, mountains
of monarchs, tiger swallowtails.

Later we lock up slowly,
reluctant to leave
the butterflies behind.

The pressmen linger, watch
me walk to my car, protective.

The next morning, they
meet me at the door –
 The new guy caught his hand in the press.
 He's at the emergency room.
We rush to the stilled machine.
I touch the terrible smashing cylinder.
A damp envelope is thrust into my hand –
 They need these.

Then a mad
dash to the hospital.
In my lap I cradle
the almost weightless fingertips
of someone
I barely know.

Morning Shift, Printing Company

Then the man who works for me, who
is my right hand, even though he is

missing half of one finger, and who lets
me know he doesn't like his job, even though

he is good at it, comes into my office with his
breakfast from 7-Eleven: a half-smoke and a Pepsi.

I think he's going to ask me, yet again,
is this how you thought you would end up?

Doing this? Instead, he tells me about his friend
Tim, the one who dropped by a few weeks ago,

his body, his face so gaunt, I didn't
recognize him. Well now, says right-hand man,

Tim's near the end. Last night, I hung out with him
so his wife could run errands. We watched

Winged Migration, have you seen it?
There aren't any actors – just birds.

It was so beautiful, we were both crying.
I was handing Tim a Kleenex

when his wife came home. She asked
me to help her in the kitchen.

*What the hell are you doing, making him
cry? It's better not to talk about it!*

I told her, the wife, we weren't talking about that,
we just cried about the movie. Then the man who

works for me unwraps his half-smoke, says, *I wonder,
do those birds have any idea where they're going?*

1968, Memorial Chapel, Ohio

Eardrums ache after Jefferson Airplane's
concert last night. Dusty balcony windows
separate us from clear light, sound. We wait
for our next class, folded into crimson
theater seats. High above us, one student
stands on the balcony railing.
                         Like a tightrope
walker, he slides the toe of his shoe along
smooth wood till his leg extends away
from his body, plants his foot, shifts his weight,
then points again. He turns his body around,
changes direction, lifts his feet as if marching.
He teeters. His arms pinwheel.
                              We are all
standing now, watching, afraid. He is beautiful.
We do nothing. We know his father is MIA,
his plane shot down in Vietnam one month ago.
We're not sure we should be sympathetic
since his father is in the military.
                               The student
stops, faces us, his arms outstretched, as if
ready to hold on to anyone with either hand.

Vietnam Summer Friends, 1969

1.

That summer's pet – a wide mouth bass.
Its fat shadow darted toward the dock,
ate worms from our hands
while we waited for AJ to
ship out to Vietnam.

AJ drove fast, too
close to parked cars, trees.
Addie and I were frightened.

An X-rated foreign movie
came to town.
AJ and Addie wanted to see it.
I asked my parents – *Is it okay?*
 You're old enough to decide yourself –
they said.
Addie and AJ and I held hands in the dark.
For a long time afterward we couldn't
call each other.

2.

That winter Addie turned
strange. She complained
> *A stegosaurus*
> *crushes my chest, won't*
> *let me out of bed.*
> *There's a whole herd of them at*
> *our old elementary school.*

My childhood dog died.

My father entered the last
year of his life.

Army doctors shipped AJ
home. I held his hand as he told me
>   *Something*
>   *exploded*
>   *and when I*
>   *came to*
>   *I was*
>   *screaming.*
>   *A log covered with*
>   *flies was near me.*
>   *It was my leg.*

3.

Today I visit the lake.
A gentle rain crawls across it –
a migration of water bugs.

I dangle my hand under the surface,
long for that shadow
to nibble my fingers again.

Cherry Tree Kabuki

Dying Higan cherries toppled – cascades
of weeping branches stacked – blossoms' white, pink
gingham chaos. Gardeners' electric
saws gnaw rotted trunks, fell our gnarled shade.
The ancient white-faced dog and I escape
our home, pass lawns scattered with ragged sink
hole graves, knotted limbs, bees hunting, frantic
for nectar. We stoop beneath realms terraced
with Akebono cherries, where Kwanzan
groves circle a still pond. The dog drinks, whorls
of pastel petals drift down, their tiny
tsunamis ripple, create water fronds.
In that pool's mirror, memory unfurls.
The dog and I watch, stricken Kabuki.

Our Frozen Forest Walk

The dog, quick
in the cold, paws' fetlocks
flicked precisely, he could
be on parade, he
is on parade, young
again. He sniffs fox,
deer scat, nothing
disgusts him.
             A rainbow-
knit cap brightens
the path ahead, its
wool stiff, something reddish
brown stains it. I warn
the dog –
        Don't you touch that –
but he prances past,
his dressage passage intent
on a granite boulder – fungus
freckled green, wrinkled black –
how can fungus live
on this frigid stone?
            The dog
stops, sniffs invisible
history: yesterday,
a common blackbird
scampered across this rock.
Is anything common?

Scar in the Moon

This is the time of year
to chase the moon down
beneath dogwood blossoms
terraced white in the moonlight.

This is the time of year
to howl, wild
at the moon,
hurl yourself toward another,
crazy for just this night.

That was before.

Now the dog and I limp upstairs,
find you naked by the window.
I kiss the scar on your back.

Shaped like a water bug, it
quivers across a moonlit lake.

The Dog Hates Storms

All night the dog kept us awake
as he barked –
inconsolable, comfortless –
the thunder, the violent summer storm.

Early this morning we survey the damaged garden –
toppled tomato plants, bruised basil,
an old nest flung on top of the hosta.

The dog and I emerge from beds
dappled with damp blossoms.
I brush them away

like I want to erase your ragged scar –
that fresh ropy line severing your life in two.

Perhaps tonight the dog and I will dream,
the dog's paws twitching.
We'll chase after you –
grab you from the edge –

or perhaps we will not be able to sleep
for the sound of thunder.

Overnight Maples Turn into Pumpkins

And the dog disappears for hours in his leaf-filled yard,
herds squirrels corner to corner.
No acorn will be harvested on his watch.

Too tired for his nighttime walk,
he puts himself to bed at eight.

Tonight as the sun sets,
wasps race to their nest,
angry that their time is almost over.
Seven deer tiptoe single file
from their feeding ground to their sleeping ground.

A full moon
shines silver on the batwing begonias.

And then it happens –
You are there –
The dog, overjoyed,
brings his ball, his stick –
anything to keep you.

It's like that other sunset –
For a long time
you had been too ill to look out the window.
Suddenly you saw the tops of the oaks –
they glowed yellow –
You asked
    How can I bear such beauty?

Last Walk

Our old dog struggled past me,
past the last line of summer.

Quicksilver butterflies fluttered
resurrected by his slow pace –
a nervous diaphanous veil
about his head.

Was he was a Bride of Christ that day?
Was he to be married to a new life?
Could he know
his walk away from us
would signal a long harsh winter –
a winter when butterflies
never danced around my ankles?

September — Arlington, Virginia

A long time ago.
Near the end.
Our old dog limped
through fallen mayapples
beside Windy Run.
Each night I brushed him,
checked for new lumps,
asked *Is tomorrow the day?*
His paws smelled like cider.

That last day he stood
still for a long time,
looked toward children
in the park, then
followed me to the car.

Each night I listened —
helicopters thumped
up and down the Potomac,
fighter jets roared
high, invisible even
when I could see
the stars. When it
rained they sounded
muffled, close.

All night long important
people were making
important decisions.

Acknowledgments

Grateful acknowledgment to the editors of the following journals and anthologies in which these poems, or versions of them, first appeared:

Apple Valley Review: "In Search of Warm Breathing Things," "Solving for the Unknown," "Past Tense"

The Broadkill Review: "Inside a Coffee Shop," "Nature's Cadenza," "Near Meander River, Near Miletus," "Now, Four Blizzards"

Chronicle of Higher Education: "Cherry Tree Kabuki"

Cobalt Review: "Butterfly Poster, Printing Company," "September – Arlington, Virginia"

Last Call: The Anthology of Beer, Wine & Spirits Poetry: "Alcohol Beckons Constantly, Derails"

Little Patuxent Review: "Rutting Fall"

Northern Virginia Review: "Beluga Pangaea," "Ice Waterfall," "Smoke," "Time Will Tell" (published as "Untitled")

Panoply: "Midnight Garden Walk, Key West"

Poetry South: "The World Trembles, The World Masquerades"

She Writes: Visions and Voices of Seaside Scribes: "Beluga Pangaea" (reprinted)

Whistling Fire: "Refracted Light"

Thank you also to the following sheet-music publishers:

Keiser Southern Music: "To Cast a Shadow Again"

Musik Fabrik Musik Publishing: "Chasing the Moon Down" (series includes "The Dog Hates Storms," "Ice Waterfall," "Overnight Maples Turn into Pumpkins," "Scar in the Moon")

Special thanks to:

Ami Kaye and everyone at Glass Lyre Press for your enthusiastic response to this manuscript;

Writing teachers Ellen Bass, Marie Howe, Gerry LaFemina, and Rose Solari;

Poetry Grrls: Lawrence Biemiller, J.K. Daniels, Martha Kreiner,

Michelle Mandolia, Karen Murph, Mariah Burton Nelson, and Katherine Williams;

Poets Meet on Fridays group;

Composers Carson Cooman and Eric Ewazen for setting two cycles of these poems to music;

Katherine J. Williams for cover artwork;

Lianna Gekker for the author photo;

Jason Gekker for author-photo advice and file preparation;

Chris Gekker, for a lifetime of unwavering support;

so many other family members and friends for your encouragement and interest in my work;

and especially to Mariah Burton Nelson: thank you to infinity and beyond.

About the Author

Katherine Gekker's poems have appeared in *Little Patuxent Review, Delmarva Review, Broadkill Review, Apple Valley Review,* and elsewhere. Her poetry has been nominated for the Pushcart Prize and Best of the Net.

Gekker founded a commercial printing company in 1974 and sold it 31 years later.

When not writing, she practices piano.

In Search of Warm Breathing Things is her first book.

Glass Lyre Press

exceptional works to replenish the spirit

Glass Lyre Press is an independent literary publisher interested in technically accomplished, stylistically distinct, and original work. Glass Lyre seeks diverse writers that possess a dynamic aesthetic and an ability to emotionally and intellectually engage a wide audience of readers.

Glass Lyre's vision is to connect the world through language and art. We hope to expand the scope of poetry and short fiction for the general reader through exceptionally well-written books, which evoke emotion, provide insight, and resonate with the human spirit.

Poetry Collections
Poetry Chapbooks
Select Short & Flash Fiction
Anthologies

www.GlassLyrePress.com

www.ingramcontent.com/pod-product-compliance
Lightning Source LLC
Chambersburg PA
CBHW030131100526
44591CB00009B/606